TEACHING
the
SCIENTIFIC
METHOD

Instructional Strategies
to Boost Student Understanding

by Millie J. Blandford

Incentive Publications, Inc.
Nashville, Tennessee

Illustrated by Marta J. Drayton
Cover by Geoffrey Brittingham
Edited by Patience Camplair

ISBN 978-0-86530-635-6

7   8   9   10   11   10

Printed by Sheridan Books, Inc., Chelsea, Michigan • *July 2010*
www.incentivepublications.com

Table of Contents

Review, Tests, and Projects

Appendix

INTRODUCTION

Scientific inquiry is a major component of the National Science Education Standards. This book is designed to help teachers deliver this concept to 5th, 6th, 7th, and 8th grade students, and the included activities and lessons can be adapted for other grade levels as well. It is designed so that you can select and use those which best meet your students' individual needs or use them together as a complete guide to the steps of the scientific method (see page 59).

As a means of introducing scientific inquiry, some "Opening Demonstrations" follow on pages 10-15 that will awaken the minds of your students and and peak their interest in scientific principles and processes. Before exploring the scientific method, however, it is essential that your students understand how to give and follow detailed directions. Therefore, we have included some activities that will drive home the importance of precision and clarity in scientific experimentation before examining each step of the process.

The activities in this book engage students in active learning. It is organized in a manner that makes daily or weekly lesson plans easy to develop. To teach any science class effectively, it is necessary to use a variety of teaching strategies such as individual assignments, group activities, in-class and at-home projects, and hands-on activities. *Teaching the Scientific Method* presents these strategies to implement in your classroom.

This book will enable students to explore each step of the scientific method so they will be successful in using it for experimentation, science fairs, and state or national tests. With this instructional tool, you will enable your students to do the following:

- solve problems using the scientific method

- conduct scientific research

- use scientific equipment appropriately

- construct, understand, and explain tables, charts, graphs, and reports

- develop experiments independently

DEMONSTRATIONS,
DIRECTIONS,
and the
STEPS OF THE METHOD

Demonstrations

Demonstrations, especially at the beginning of the year, are an effective way to motivate students and grab their attention. After the demonstration, lead a discussion about the scientific concept behind it. Using these at the beginning of the year will help you gauge student understanding and prior knowledge; they will also break the ice and help students feel comfortable. If used later in the year, these demonstrations will provide a refreshing break from the routine for both teachers and students.

CAN CRUSH

Materials:

empty soda cans, a pair of tongs, a hot plate, a small amount of water, and a medium to large bowl of ice water

Procedure:

1. Turn the hot plate on high.

2. Put a couple of tablespoons of water in the can, and set it on the burner.

3. When most or all of the water has boiled out of the can, use the tongs to grab the can and quickly flip it upside down in the ice water. The greater the temperature difference, the larger the "BOOM".

Science behind the demonstration:

When molecules are heated, they move quickly and spread out. Heating the can enables the air molecules to escape from the can. Flipping the can upside down in the ice water prevents more air molecules from moving into the can. When the can is cooled down quickly, the molecules of the can, and any air that is left, will rapidly slow their movement and contract. Since there is now more air on the outside of the can than on the inside, the pressure of the outside air crushes the can.

BALLOON IN A JAR

Materials:

a gallon-size pickle jar, a water balloon (a bit larger than the opening of the jar), tissues, a lighter, and a thick straw

Procedure:

1. Fill the balloon with water so that it is large enough to sit on top of the jar without sliding in.

2. Ask the students how you will get the balloon into the jar without popping it. Ask them what is in the jar that is keeping the balloon from going in. Ask them how you can get the air out of the jar.

3. Remove the balloon from the top of the jar, light a piece of tissue, and put it in the bottom of the jar.

4. Quickly place the balloon back on top of the jar and watch what happens.

5. To remove the balloon, hold onto the straw with one hand and put it part way down into the jar. With the other hand, pull the balloon out. Do not let the straw bend.

Science behind the demonstration:

Again, molecules move quickly and spread out when they are heated. As the balloon bounces up and down on top of the jar, some of the air is being removed from the jar. The oxygen in the air is being used up by the fire. Once the air is out of the jar, the balloon creates a type of vacuum. The students will think that the balloon is being sucked into the jar.

The air pressure on the outside of the jar will push the balloon in because there is more air outside of the jar than inside. To remove the balloon, more air has to go into the jar to help push it back out. The straw allows the air to move back into the jar under the balloon to help push it out.

Caution: Do not use the same balloon more than three times.

HOLE IN THE WATER BOTTLE

Materials:

a 16–20 ounce soda or water bottle with a top, a sharp object such as a compass, and water

Procedure:

1. Use the sharp object to poke a hole through the bottle about 3 cm from the bottom (it may also work with the hole on the bottom).
2. Fill the bottle almost completely with water, holding your finger over the hole.
3. Replace the top and hold the bottle from the top.
4. Do not hold the sides of the bottle or squeeze it.
5. Slowly unscrew the top and watch the water pour out of the hole.

Science behind the demonstration:

There is enough air pressure outside of the bottle to hold the water in when the top is secured. When the top is loosened, more air is able to move into the bottle, pushing the water out through the hole.

Teaching the Scientific Method

HAMMER AND RULER

Materials:

a hammer, a wooden ruler, a string about 20–25 cm (8 to 10 inches) long, and a table or other flat surface

Procedure:

1. Tie the string end to end so that you have a loop. The trick to getting this to work is the length of the string, so you may have to adjust the length (approximately 5–7 cm or 2–3 in. in diameter).

2. Put the ruler and the head of the hammer through the string, with the ruler above the hammer.

3. The string should be toward the end of the ruler at about the 5–7 cm or 2–3 inch mark.

4. Holding both the ruler and hammer, place the short section of the ruler (5–7 cm or 2–3 inches) on a flat surface (such as a thin tabletop) that has nothing under it.

5. Let go of the hammer and ruler, and watch your toes! It may take you several tries before you are able to easily suspend the hammer under the ruler.

6. The head of the hammer should be hanging down toward the floor and the handle of the hammer should be touching the center of the ruler. If done correctly, it is possible to have only 2 or 3 mm ($\frac{1}{4}$ in.) of the ruler on the tabletop. The hammer will stay suspended under the ruler as long as nothing touches it.

Science behind the demonstration:

The hammer stays suspended under the ruler because its center of gravity is located directly under the base of the ruler.

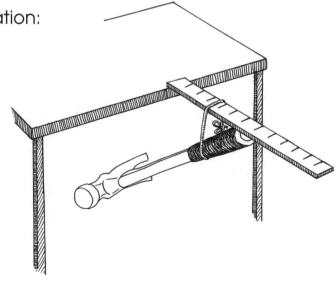

TISSUE AND CUP

Materials:

a clear plastic cup, a tissue, and a clear container of water

Procedure:

1. Place the tissue in the bottom of the cup.

2. Flip the cup upside down and push it straight down in the water.

3. Pulling the cup straight up, lift it out of the water and remove the tissue. It should remain dry.

Science behind the demonstration:

When the cup goes straight down into the water, the air in the cup does not escape; therefore, the air between the tissue and the water acts as a barrier so the water cannot reach the tissue. If the cup is tilted going in or coming out of the water, the air will escape, and the tissue will get wet.

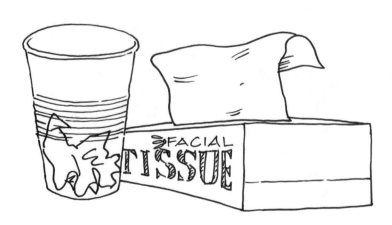

CUP WON'T BURN

Materials:

two paper cups, a ring stand, a pair of tongs, a container of water, and a flame

Procedure:

1. Put the first empty cup on the ring stand, suspended a little over the flame.

2. Time how long it takes the cup to catch on fire.

3. Use the tongs to remove the burning cup and quickly put it in the container of water.

4. Next, fill the other cup $\frac{1}{3}$ to $\frac{1}{2}$ full of water and place it in the ring stand, over the flame. Time how long it takes it to catch on fire.

Science behind the demonstration:

The first cup catches on fire much more quickly than the second cup. The water in the second cup is a better conductor of heat than the paper from which the cup is made. The heat from the flame warms up the water inside the cup before it heats the paper because paper is an insulator. Insulators are not good conductors of heat. The first cup did not contain a conductor to pull the heat from the flame because air is also an insulator.

Directions:
Building a Good Foundation

FOLLOWING DIRECTIONS

It is important that students follow directions in any class, although this is especially true in science because of the potential dangers involved with materials and equipment. Furthermore, it is important to know how to follow and give clear, precise, and detailed directions when performing or writing up an experiment. An experiment should be designed with detailed instructions so that it can be easily followed. This insures that others can perform the exact experiment without questioning the procedure.

Copy and distribute the "Following Directions" handout on page 17 for this activity.

Procedure:

1. Hand out the copies of "Following Directions" to students, and set a 3-minute time limit for the activity.

2. Remind students to read the directions to themselves before beginning.

3. When the time is up, read the directions and the numbered items aloud.

4. Identify those who actually followed the directions, and discuss the importance of following directions in a science lab.

Notes:

_____

_____

_____

FOLLOWING DIRECTIONS

Directions: This exercise tests how well you follow directions. You have 3 minutes to complete the task. First read all 20 items, and then do exactly as you are instructed.

1. Write your name in the space provided at the top of the paper.

2. Write the date in the top right corner of the paper.

3. Write your best friend's name in the bottom right corner of the paper.

4. Count to ten on your fingers, out loud.

5. Say "boogity" out loud 5 times.

6. Stand up and turn around 3 times.

7. Shake the hand of the person on either side of you.

8. Clap your hands 5 times.

9. Blink your eyes and touch your nose 10 times.

10. Take off your shoes and wiggle your toes.

11. Stand up and say 3 times out loud "I love broccoli!".

12. Lay your head on your desk for 10 seconds.

13. Put your shoes back on your feet.

14. Write your teacher's name in the bottom left corner of the paper.

15. Scratch your head and rub your belly for 10 seconds.

16. Stand up and sing, "Mary Had a Little Lamb".

17. Do 5 jumping jacks.

18. Write your favorite holiday on the back of the paper.

19. Sing your favorite song out loud.

20. Do not do any of the activities after number 2.
    Turn your paper over when you finish.

Teaching the Scientific Method

GIVING DIRECTIONS TO OTHERS

Listening skills are a big factor in following directions. Lead your students in this activity and discuss the importance of listening. Ask students how they can improve listening and directing skills.

Materials:

paper and pencil

Procedure:

1. List seven activities on a sheet of paper, and read through all of them aloud without stopping.

2. Do not repeat the list, and do not allow students to write the items down.

3. Have students take turns trying to perform the activities in the exact order that they were given.

Example: 1. Do five jumping jacks in front of the class.

2. Go to the back of the room and turn around 3 times.

3. Shake the hand of the person closest to you.

4. Look out the right rear window.

5. Sing "I'm a Little Tea Pot" on the right side of the room.

6. Sit in the teacher's chair for five seconds.

7. Write the date on the board.

4. Continue with the exercise until someone is able to complete it.
   Next, have students write their own directions for others to follow.

Notes:

_____

_____

_____

_____

BLINDFOLD DIRECTIONS

This is another activity designed to help with listening skills. Before trying it out with students, review what they have learned about giving and listening to directions. After the activity, discuss what made the directions easy or difficult to follow.

Materials:

handkerchief to use as a blindfold

Procedure:

1. Blindfold one student.

2. Have others, one at a time, give the blindfolded student directions to a specific destination in the room.

3. Emphasize the importance of giving clear, precise, and detailed directions.

4. Stay close to the student in case he or she needs some assistance stepping over objects.

Challenge your students by setting up obstacles, such as chairs or stacks of books.

Notes:

_____

_____

_____

_____

_____

_____

_____

_____

Writing the Problem

The problem is the first step of the scientific method. It is a testable question, and should be written in question form. Only one variable at a time should be tested so that the results can be easily clarified. You may also wish to teach the concepts of research, demonstrations, and models at this time, emphasizing how they differ from testable problems.

Definitions:

Test—An attempt to solve a problem through experimentation. This is also called an experiment or an investigation. To verify results, an actual test should be conducted at least three times or should contain at least three samples of items to test (see "Examples of Testable Problems", page 21). A test shows why and how something works or reacts the way it does.

Research—Information about an idea obtained through observations, surveys, the Internet, books, or other sources to answer a question. Asking someone which brand of deodorant works best is research, not a test. Setting up the experiment and having individuals try different kinds of deodorant is a test.

Demonstration—A demonstration uses an example or illustrates a series of steps to show how something works. It does not explain why it works. A test attempts to show both.

Model—A model is closely related to the demonstration. Emphasizing the pattern or makeup of the object in question, a model shows its design, but does not explain why it works the way it does. Models can be used in demonstrations and tests; however, to be classified as a test, it must provide for experimentation and measurable results.

> **Note:** *The difference in a model and demonstration may be difficult to distinguish. A model usually shows the makeup, while a demonstration shows a process. Whenever you have a demonstration, it can also be categorized as a model. You may wish to teach these two concepts as one.*

EXAMPLES OF TESTABLE PROBLEMS

1. Which flavor of gum lasts the longest?

2. Which brand of laundry detergent is best at getting rid of stains?

3. Which brand of toilet paper is the strongest?

4. Who can hit the most free throws in ten tries?

5. What is the effect of cigarette smoke on household plants?

6. How many styrofoam peanuts will react in $\frac{1}{3}$ cup of acetone?

7. How many times will the top pop off of the film canister?

8. In a natural filtration system, how should rocks, sand, and dirt be layered to get the cleanest water?

9. Who can last the longest doing the "Phantom Chair"?

10. How many pennies can fit in a cup full of water without it overflowing?

11. Do dogs see in color?

12. How does exercise affect the heart rate?

13. What factor causes mold to grow on bread the quickest?

14. What effect does temperature change have on any given substance?

15. Which battery size will light the most light bulbs?

Emphasize the importance of testing only one variable at a time. If the word "best" is used in the questions, clarify what this means.

After going over these examples, have students come up with their own problems to test.

1. Group students or have them individually write testable problems.

2. Share these as a class so students can put them in their notes for further reference.

Notes:

_____

_____

_____

Conducting Research

Research may give students an idea for an experiment or allow students to better understand the content of an experiment by helping them form a hypothesis. Learning to conduct research at the middle grades level prepares students for the requirements of later education. To familiarize students with the process of research, have them investigate ideas using books, the Internet, or surveys. The students also learn how to pick out key words in a "problem" to research.

Ideas for Research:

1. Surveys that reveal popularity or effectiveness of products (best tasting, etc.)

2. Surveys that reveal beliefs about ideas

3. Information about products from manufacturers (usually can be found on commercials or on the packaging)

4. Information that gives details about materials used in the experiment. For example: What is acetone? What are its uses?

Before they begin investigating, discuss the concept of "key words" with your students so that they know how to spot key words in the problem they want to research. Some examples follow.

Problem: What causes mold to grow on bread?

Key Words: mold and bread

Problem: If I exercise strenuously for 15 minutes per day, how long will it take to lower my resting heart rate 3 beats per minute?

Key Words: exercise and resting heart rate

TEST, RESEARCH, DEMONSTRATION, OR MODEL?

Materials:

Copy and use the handout on page 23 for this activity.

Procedure:

1. Students may work in groups or individually to complete the task.

2. They must identify each as a test, research, demonstration, or model.

TEST, RESEARCH, DEMONSTRATION, OR MODEL?

Identify each problem below as a test, research, demonstration, or model. Be prepared to explain why you made each choice you did.

_____ 1. How does a volcano erupt?

_____ 2. What is your favorite brand of jeans?

_____ 3. Which brand of tissue is the strongest?

_____ 4. Why doesn't water come out of the hole in bottle?

_____ 5. Why doesn't the paper cup burn?

_____ 6. Which order will the liquids stack on top of one another from most dense to least dense?

_____ 7. Which foods contain an acid?

_____ 8. How do you clean up an acid?

_____ 9. How does a circuit work?

_____ 10. What is the difference in a parallel and a series circuit?

_____ 11. Which flavor of gum do most people say will last the longest?

_____ 12. How does the balloon get in the jar?

_____ 13. Which foods eaten just before bedtime cause you to dream more?

_____ 14. How many planets are in our solar system?

_____ 15. How far away is Jupiter?

_____ 16. Which types of foods contain starch?

_____ 17. How many different microorganisms are found in a dropper full of pond water?

_____ 18. How small is Pluto compared to the other planets?

_____ 19. How is toothpaste made?

_____ 20. Who do you think will win the next election?

Teaching the Scientific Method

23

QUIZ

Test, Research, Demonstration, or Model?

An actual scientific problem can be solved only through experimentation. Demonstrations, models, or research are not experiments, but they are used in experiments.
(*Tests*, *experiments*, and *investigations* are words that can be used interchangeably.)

Definitions:

1. **Model**—a display of an object that merely shows *what that object looks like*. Often used in tests and demonstrations.

2. **Demonstration**—a model or display that shows *how something works*, but does not test anything.

3. **Research**—scientific information gathered through observations, surveys, or other sources *to explain a problem*; no test is conducted.

4. **Test**—the gathering of data in which a variable is used and everything is controlled to stay constant except for the one variable that you are testing (also referred to as an experiment or investigation).

Determine whether each of the following problems is a demonstration, model, research, or test. Fill in the blank with the correct term.

1. _____ Of what is a molecule made?

2. _____ Which types of food contain starch?

3. _____ How do stalactites and stalagmites form?

4. _____ How far away is lightning?

5. _____ What causes mold to grow on bread?

6. _____ How fast does the Earth rotate?

7. _____ Which brand of sneakers allows you to jump the highest?

8. _____ How does a volcano work?

9. _____ Which type of fruit tree produces the most fruit?

10. _____ Which soft drink stays fizzy the longest?

Developing a Hypothesis

A hypothesis is an educated guess, based on research or general knowledge, that is developed before an experiment is conducted. In order to teach scientific writing, require students to write a hypothesis as an "If . . . , then . . ." statement. Phrases such as "I think . . .", "I believe . . .", "I predict . . ." should not be used. If items being tested are not written in the problem, then they must be written in the hypothesis.

Stress that if a hypothesis is wrong after the experiment is completed, that does not indicate that the experiment was a failure. Some great ideas and inventions have resulted from incorrect hypotheses. Just as much knowledge, if not more, can be gained from an incorrect hypothesis as from a correct one. Begin this lesson with a few prediction activities (see pages 26 and 27).

Examples of Problems and Hypotheses:

1. What is the effect of cigarette smoke on household plants?
   If I test to see how cigarette smoke affects household plants,
   then it will _____.

2. How many styrofoam peanuts will dissolve in ⅓ cup of acetone?
   If I test to determine how many peanuts will dissolve in the acetone,
   then it will be _____.

3. In a natural filtration system, how should rocks, sand, and dirt be layered to get the cleanest water?
   If I test to see how the materials should be layered,
   then their order from top to bottom will be _____.

4. Do dogs see in color?
   If I test a dogs' ability to see in color,
   then they _____.

5. How does exercise affect the heart rate?
   If I test to determine how exercise affects the heart rate,
   then it will _____.

PRACTICE WRITING A HYPOTHESIS

Directions: Write a hypothesis for each problem below using an "If . . . , then . . ." statement. Do not write "I think . . . " or any similar phrase.

> **Example:** Which is a more effective heat source, coal, natural gas, or electricity?
>
> If I test to see which provides warmest heat in the shortest time, then it will be natural gas.

1. Which brand of soap gets rid of germs the best?

   _____

   _____

2. What is the best amount of sunlight and water for growing violets?

   _____

   _____

3. Which brand of sneakers will allow you to jump the highest?

   _____

   _____

4. How many pounds of weight can be held by a bridge made out of 30 popsicle sticks?

   _____

   _____

5. How are student grades affected by the amount of time spent viewing television?

   _____

   _____

PREDICTION BOX

Materials:

a small box, tape, a small object such as a marble, marker, coin, etc.

Procedure:

1. First, discuss methods used to make predictions—gathering research and/or observations using all of our senses.

2. Put an object in the box.

3. Tape the top and bottom together so that students cannot open it.

4. Pass the box around the room, and direct students to make observations about the object inside the box based on senses other than sight. It may be helpful to make several boxes containing the same object to save time.

5. After everyone has observed the box, each student should write down his or her prediction of the mystery object's identity.

6. Allow students to share their predictions, and open the box.

Notes:

_____

_____

_____

_____

_____

_____

_____

_____

_____

DISSOLVING PEANUTS

This is a prediction demonstration that usually amazes students.

Materials:

styrofoam peanuts, highly concentrated acetone (more strongly concentrated than fingernail polish), an opaque glass coffee mug

Procedure:

1. Gather lots of styrofoam packing peanuts at the beginning of the year. Use peanuts that have a smooth texture.

2. Before the students arrive, pour $\frac{1}{3}$ to $\frac{1}{2}$ cup of acetone in the coffee mug. The acetone can be purchased at any hardware store. It evaporates quickly, so do not let it sit too long.

3. Discuss the concept of prediction with your students.

4. Have each student write on a sheet of paper their prediction of how many styrofoam peanuts will fit in the cup. Do not tell students that there is anything in the cup.

5. Start putting the peanuts in the cup, counting as you go. If you have done this before, you know that you will soon get tired of counting and the students will take over. They will also quickly realize that something must have already been in the cup. A chemical reaction occurs between the peanuts and the acetone.

6. When you are tired of dropping in the peanuts (or if you have run out), share your secret.

7. Save the cup so students can see the compacted peanuts.

Notes:

_____

_____

_____

_____

Writing the Materials List

The materials list should be written in list form, with each item numbered. All materials or substances, their amounts, and any needed equipment must be included.

Here is an example, using a familiar experiment:

Materials List:

1. 1500 (or more) styrofoam peanuts
2. Can of acetone (any size)
3. $\frac{1}{3}$ cup measuring cup
4. One opaque coffee mug

Try another example with your students.

1. Have them write a materials list for the ingredients and materials used to make an ice cream sundae.
2. Share their lists as a class to make sure nothing has been left out and that everyone has included the correct amounts.

For a homework assignment, have students write a materials list for their favorite recipe.

Notes:

_____

_____

_____

_____

_____

Writing the Procedure

The procedure should be written in list form, with each step numbered. This makes it much easier to follow. Clear, precise, and detailed directions should be given in each step. Since the amounts of the materials are to be written in the "Materials List", you do not have to repeat the amounts in this section.

Remind students of the importance of giving good directions. Others must be able to easily follow their experiment exactly, without questioning any part of it.

Example:

Steps for "Dissolving Peanuts" Procedure:

1. Gather all materials.

2. Before the students arrive, pour $\frac{1}{3}$ cup of acetone into the coffee mug.

3. Do not let anyone see the acetone in the cup.

4. Have students write the number of styrofoam peanuts they predict will fit into the cup.

5. Allow students to share their predictions.

6. Begin putting peanuts into the cup one at a time, counting out loud as you do so.

7. Continue putting the peanuts into the coffee mug until you get tired or run out of peanuts.

8. Share your secret.

MAKING A PEANUT BUTTER SANDWICH

Materials:

jar of peanut butter, loaf of bread, butter knife, paper plates, paper towels, crackers

Procedure:

1. Have the students, one at a time, give you a step of the directions for making a peanut butter sandwich.

2. The key to this is to follow the direction *exactly* as it is given. If they say, "Open the bread," without offering any details, then rip open the plastic bag. Bread will fall everywhere, but it gets the point across. Spend about 15–20 minutes on this demonstration. You will probably create a mess and a lot of laughter, but it teaches the students that the directions need to be clear, precise, and detailed.

3. After you have accomplished the task of making a peanut butter sandwich, make peanut butter and crackers to share as a class. As your students enjoy the snack, discuss how to improve the sandwich-making directions.

Notes:

_____

_____

_____

_____

_____

_____

_____

_____

_____

PAPER CLIP DESIGN

Materials:

paper clips of many different colors (enough for each person to have about eight), and dividers to place between students, such as binders or books

Procedure:

1. Students must work with a partner for this activity.

2. Pass out the same number and the same colors of paper clips to each partner.

3. Students must put some sort of divider between themselves and their partner.

4. One partner will begin by picking up a paper clip and placing it on the table, without the other partner seeing it.

5. After the paper clip has been placed, he or she will tell the partner its color and clearly direct him or her about of how to place it on the table or desk in exactly the same way.

6. The person giving the directions must also write the directions (clear, precise, and detailed) on a sheet of paper that will be handed in later and graded.

7. All of the paper clips must be used to create a design. Designs should be something other than a straight row of paper clips. Encourage your students to be creative.

8. The direction giver must not at any time tell what the shape will look like. Clues should be used such as North, South, East, West, top, bottom, left, right, vertically, horizontally, and diagonally.

9. The person receiving directions cannot ask questions. He or she must simply follow the directions as they are given, to the best of their understanding.

10. Once the design has been completed and the directions have been written down, check the students' work. Ask the person who received directions if the directions were easy or difficult to follow. Remove the divider. If directions were clear, the designs should be identical.

11. Put the divider back in place so the other partner can create a design.

12. Before turning in the written directions, have the students draw sketches of their designs and label the paper clip colors.

Notes:

_____

_____

_____

Collecting Data: Observation Skills

The sixth step of the scientific method is data collection. Collecting data requires observations. When we think about observations, most of us automatically think of the sense of sight, since that is the sense we most often use when we observe; however, scientific observations will most likely require the use of the other senses as well.

Discuss the five senses as they relate to observation skills. You will need several materials for this activity. The following is merely a list of suggestions.

Smell — Have students smell and identify odors, such as extracts. Explain to students that never are they to smell anything in the lab unless told to do so. Teach them the proper way to smell science materials by waving the odor toward their noses.

Touch — Put a variety of small objects in an opaque bag and have students feel the objects to identify as many as possible.

Hearing — Have students listen to others' voices in the room and try to identify each person. You may also play the game with students trying to disguise their voices instead.

Taste — **First make it clear that nothing is to be tasted in the lab unless students are instructed to do so.** Blindfold one student at a time, and have him or her taste various substances such as salt, sugar, extracts, chocolate, etc.

Sight — Observe a peanut in its shell. Make a detailed list of characteristics such as color, size, mass, and distinguishing marks. Next, have the students describe in writing how it smells, feels, sounds, and tastes.

Notes:

_____

_____

_____

_____

_____

CHANGE IS IN THE AIR

This activity allows students to use their sense of sight.

Procedure:

1. Choose 4 to 6 students at a time to participate.

2. Have these students come to the front of the class.

3. Pick another student to be the observer.

4. Tell the observer to carefully examine everything about the students who are in front of the class.

5. After a minute or two, dismiss the observer from the room.

6. Next, have the participants quickly make a few changes to their appearance. Possible changes may include trading shoes with others in the class, adding jewelry, removing jewelry, changing hairstyles, and so on. The kids can get really creative with this.

7. After everyone has quickly made their changes, bring the observer back into the room, and see how many of the changes he or she can identify.

OR

Try a similar activity, but make changes to the room instead. Once the observer is out of the room, choose 3 or 4 students to make changes within the room. Suggestions for room changes include writing something new on the board, erasing existing information from the board, moving medium or large objects (such as a globe) to different places, switching students from their normal seats, and a favorite—changing the time on the clock.

Notes:

_____

_____

_____

_____

_____

_____

PEANUT IDENTIFICATION

Materials:

peanuts (still in the shell)

Procedure:

1. Assign students to groups of four. Give a peanut to each group, and asking them observe it in its shell.

2. Instruct them to familiarize themselves with the peanut as much as possible, without marking on or damaging it in any way.

3. Allow students about 5 minutes to observe their peanut.

4. Collect all the peanuts and place them in a pile on a table or desk, along with a few extras that did not belong to any group.

5. Let each group designate a member to identify the group's peanut. Have one representative at a time look in the pile of peanuts to find the one belonging to their group. The representative must take it back to the group to verify that it is theirs.

6. If someone in the group disagrees, they cannot exchange it until every other group has had their turn.

7. If a representative cannot find their peanut, they may send another representative or wait until all groups have gone, then look at the peanuts retrieved by the other groups.

8. If one group thinks another group has their peanut, they must persuade the class that it belongs to them.

9. Other foods that work well with this activity are cherry tomatoes, chocolate chip cookies, and small apples.

Notes:

_____

_____

_____

_____

Data Measurement and Equipment Use

To further develop data collection, obtaining and calculating measurements is crucial. The following activities teach students how to convert units within the metric system, how to measure mass, length, volume, and density, and how to effectively use the appropriate scientific equipment. They will learn how to use a triple beam balance, graduated cylinders, and metersticks/metric rulers. A solid understanding of the metric system should be encouraged through its use in scientific calculations since it is the system of measurement that is most often used in science.

LEARNING THE METRIC SYSTEM

For the first lesson, create and laminate a poster or banner that lists the metric units of measurement. It can remain on the wall all year for students to use as a reference. After reviewing the basic units, work as a group to practice converting units within the metric system. Spend quite a bit of time on this activity to make sure everyone understands the concept, since the activities that follow require the students to perform metric conversions. Remind the students of the three simple steps to follow when converting units within the metric system:

> (1) Look at the unit you are starting with.
>
> (2) See which unit you need to go to.
>
> (3) Move the decimal that many spaces in the same direction.

After students become familiar with metric units, try this activity.

MEASURING UNITS OF LENGTH

Materials:

metric rulers and metersticks, copies of the handouts on pages 37 & 38

Procedure:

1. Distribute metersticks and metric rulers to each student, along with a copy of pages 37 and 38.

2. Allow students to complete this activity in groups.

3. Each group must find ten items to measure in centimeters. Students especially enjoy taking this activity outside. The following day, the students convert their measurements to other units.

MEASURING LENGTH IN METRICS

Instructions: Identify ten objects and measure them in centimeters. Each line on your ruler represents a millimeter (mm), and each number represents a centimeter (cm). Always include your units.

Name/Description of Object   Measurement in cm

1. _____   _____

2. _____   _____

3. _____   _____

4. _____   _____

5. _____   _____

6. _____   _____

7. _____   _____

8. _____   _____

9. _____   _____

10. _____   _____

METRIC CONVERSIONS (LENGTH)

Instructions: Convert the length measurements to meters and one other metric unit of your choice (Km, Hm, Dam, dm, cm, or mm). Remember: 1) Look at the unit you are starting with. 2) See which unit you are going to. 3) Move the decimal the same amount of spaces in the same direction. You may show your work on the back. Always include your units.

Km	Hm	Dam	meters	dm	cm	mm
		cm		meters		other

1. _____ _____ _____

2. _____ _____ _____

3. _____ _____ _____

4. _____ _____ _____

5. _____ _____ _____

6. _____ _____ _____

7. _____ _____ _____

8. _____ _____ _____

9. _____ _____ _____

10. _____ _____ _____

MEASURING THE MASS OF OBJECTS

Materials:

triple beam balances, digital scales, small objects, and copies of page 40, "Measuring and Converting Mass"

Procedure:

1. First, discuss the difference in mass and weight, which is sometimes a difficult concept to grasp. Mass is the amount of matter in an object, and weight is the amount of gravitational pull on an object.

2. Next, practice as a group the proper use of the triple beam balance.

3. Divide students into small groups so everyone will have a chance to use the triple beam balances.

4. Instruct each group to find the mass of five different objects in the room—three using the triple beam balance and the other two using the digital scales.

5. If time allows, students should use the digital scales to check the measurements of the objects measured with the triple beam balances.

6. After they get their measurements, have students convert the measurements from grams to other units within the metric system.

Notes:

_____

_____

_____

_____

_____

_____

_____

_____

MEASURING AND CONVERTING MASS

Instructions: Using the triple beam balance, measure the mass of three different objects, and then measure the mass of the remaining 2 objects on the digital scales. When you are finished, convert to the units indicated below. Always include your units.

Remember—triple beam Balance directions:

1). Make sure every weight, and the beam, is on zero.

2). Move the 100's weight first, one slot at a time. When it drops below zero, move it back one space.

3). Next, move the 10's weight, one slot at a time. When it drops below zero, move it back one slot.

4). Lastly, slowly move the 1's weight until the beam is set on zero.

5). Add the weights in the order that they were moved. Record totals below.

Kg   Hg   Dag   grams   dg   cg   mg

Mass in Grams   Other Unit Conversions

1. _____   _____ Kg

2. _____   _____ mg

3. _____   _____ Dag

4. _____   _____ dg

5. _____   _____ Hg

MEASURING AND CONVERTING VOLUME

Materials:

graduated cylinders, water, small objects such as marbles, bolts, washers, screws, metric rulers, and copies of pages 42 and 43

Procedure:

1. First, teach students how to read a graduated cylinder.

2. Review the steps for measuring the volume of a liquid and the volume of an irregularly shaped object.

3. After practicing with the graduated cylinder as a group, practice calculating volume of a regularly shaped object (L x W x H) with metric rulers.

4. Place students in small groups to conduct their own measurements and conversions.

Notes:

_____

_____

_____

_____

_____

_____

_____

_____

_____

_____

_____

MEASURING AND CONVERTING VOLUME

Instructions: Use the graduated cylinder to measure the volume of five irregularly shaped objects. Next, use the metric ruler or meterstick to calculate the volume of five regularly shaped objects. Once you have taken all your measurements, convert the units. Always include your units. (A graduated cylinder is measured in ml, and units for regularly shaped objects are cm^3 or m^3.)

Name of Irregularly Shaped Objects   Volume of Objects

1. _____   _____

2. _____   _____

3. _____   _____

4. _____   _____

5. _____   _____

Name of Regularly Shaped Objects   Volume of Objects

1. _____   _____

2. _____   _____

3. _____   _____

4. _____   _____

5. _____   _____

Name_____ Date_____

CONVERSION OF VOLUME UNITS

Instructions: Convert the volume measurements to the units shown below. Always include your units. (Remember: 1 ml = 1 cm^3)

Kl   Hl   Dal   liters   dl   cl   ml

Volume of Irregularly Shaped Objects   Conversions

1. _____   _____ liters

2. _____   _____ Kl

3. _____   _____ dl

4. _____   _____ liters

5. _____   _____ Hl

Km   Hm   Dam   meters   dm   cm   mm

Volume of Regularly Shaped Objects   Conversions

1. _____   _____ m^3

2. _____   _____ Km^3

3. _____   _____ dm^3

4. _____   _____ ml

5. _____   _____ liters

Teaching the Scientific Method

Density Demonstrations

Density is often a hard concept for students to comprehend. Students may understand it most clearly as some objects are "heavy" and some are "light". The formula for density is Density = Mass/Volume (D = M/V) meaning, "how much mass an object has in a particular volume". The unit for density is grams per cubic centimeter or ml (g/cm^3 or g/ml). Begin this lesson with a few density demonstrations.

REGULAR AND DIET DRINK

Materials:

a large, clear container full of water, a diet soda, and regular soda

Procedure:

1. Ask the students what they think will happen when the two cans of soda are placed in the water.

2. Slowly, lower the regular soda into the water.

3. Next, place the diet soda into the water. The regular soda sinks further in the water than the diet does.

Science behind the demonstration:

The regular soda is more dense than the diet because it contains sugar. The sugar has more mass than the substitute sweetener that is in the diet drink. You can show this by using a balance scale. Add sugar to a small container, then balance the scales with a sweetener substitute. Lastly, use a digital scale or triple beam balance to get the mass of each.

SINKING THE ALUMINUM FOIL

Materials:

a large, clear container full of water, two sheets of aluminum foil the same size, and a hammer

Procedure:

1. Start the demonstration by telling the students that because the two sheets are the same size, they have the same mass and volume.

2. Discuss what might happen to density if the volume changes.

3. Wad up the two sheets into balls and drop them in the container of water.

4. Take one of the aluminum foil balls out. Begin decreasing its volume by squeezing it tightly together.

5. Drop it back into the water to see if its density has changed.

6. Take it out of the water and hammer it into a small, very compressed cube. Again, drop it back into the water.

Science behind the demonstration:

This demonstration shows that when you decrease the volume of an object, its density will increase, because it is not losing any mass.

DENSITY STACK

Materials:

tap water, highly concentrated salt water, glycerol, dark corn syrup, alcohol, 5 small plastic cups, food coloring, several test tubes or small glass graduated cylinders, test tube rack, and eyedroppers

Procedure:

1. Before the students arrive, label the cups A, B, C, D, and E and fill each about $\frac{1}{2}$ full with a different liquid. (It does not matter which liquid goes into which cup.)

2. Put a different food coloring into each liquid except the corn syrup. (It is already dark.)

3. Let the students observe the cups of liquid, and have them predict in what order of density they think the liquids will stack from top to bottom (do not tell them yet what the liquids are).

4. Choose a few predictions to demonstrate before you show them the actual results.

5. When adding the liquids, use the eyedroppers to slowly let the liquids run down the side of the test tubes or graduated cylinders. The tap water and salt water mix easily if added too quickly.

6. After trying some of the student suggestions, put the liquids into the test tube from most dense to least dense—corn syrup, glycerol, salt water, tap water, alcohol.

7. Let the students guess what they think each liquid is.

Older students may be able to perform this experiment themselves and calculate the actual densities of each liquid.

MEASURING AND CALCULATING DENSITY

Materials:

copies of page 47, as well as the objects listed there, graduated cylinders, triple beam balances, metric rulers

Procedure:

1. Set up objects and equipment around the room.

2. Group students with about 4–6 in a group.

3. Have students calculate the densities of the objects listed in the chart.

Notes:

_____

_____

_____

_____

_____

_____

_____

_____

_____

_____

_____

_____

MEASURING AND CALCULATING DENSITY

Instructions: The formula for density is Density = Mass/Volume.
Use this formula to calculate density for the objects listed below.
Always include your units. The units for density are g/cm^3 or g/ml.

OBJECT (grams)	MASS (ml or cm^3)	VOLUME (g/ml or g/cm^3)	DENSITY
1. A Small Rock			
2. Two Marbles			
3. Science Book			
4. Tissue Box			
5. Small Book			
6. Check Box			
7. 5 Pennies			
8. Small Toy Car			
9. Your choice of an irregularly shaped object			
10. Your choice of a regularly shaped object			

Using the density calculations from your chart above, list the objects and their corresponding densities in order from least dense to most dense.

1. _____   6. _____

2. _____   7. _____

3. _____   8. _____

4. _____   9. _____

5. _____   10 _____

Teaching the Scientific Method

METRICS QUIZ

Fill in each blank with the correct answer.

1. 1000 ml = _____ liters.

2. Milli- means _____.

3. One kilogram = _____ grams.

4. Kilo- means _____.

5. Liter is a measure of _____.

6. Centi- means _____.

7. Hecto- means _____.

8. Gram is a measure of _____.

9. 10 Dkm = _____ meters.

10. Deka- means _____.

11. Deci- means _____.

12. Meter measures _____.

13. Temperature in the metric system is measured by degrees _____.

14. The basic unit for distance or length in the metric system is _____.

15. The basic unit for volume
    in the metric system
    can be represented by _____, _____, _____,

Teaching the Scientific Method

Graphing Data

The final step in utilizing data is learning to create and interpret graphs. With these activities, students will learn how to make charts and tables, bar graphs, line graphs, and pie graphs. Students should be capable of using at least two different representations of data when they write up their experiments. Along with the above examples, pictures may also be used if the experiment allows for it. Students must accurately title and label each data depiction. In other words, they must indicate what the numbers, words, or pictures represent on the graphs. The metric system should be required to display data that includes measurements.

MAKING CHARTS, TABLES & GRAPHS

Materials:

drawing paper and/or graph paper, rulers, colored pencils

Procedure:

1. Familiarize students with charts and graphs by having them look at examples from their textbooks.

2. Have them copy these examples in their notes.

3. Next, direct the class to construct their own graphs. Provide information for the students to use for this step, or collect some as a class. For example, they might chart the number of family members each student has, their pets, different types of vehicles, or favorite candies.

4. When making pie graphs, assist students by calculating percentages as a group until they get they are comfortable doing this individually.

Most any information can be put into a chart, table, or bar graph. Line graphs should show a change over a period of time or a comparison such as speed. Students often think that bar and line graphs are interchangeable, but usually they are not. Pie graphs must show percentages that combine to equal 100%. (This is the most difficult graph to teach students.) Encourage students to make colored charts and graphs, and to use rulers to make them as neatly as possible.

Teaching the Scientific Method

Examples: All of the following information is hypothetical. Students may use this information about grades to construct their charts and graphs. Or, the class can brainstorm their own data.

Students' Grades

5 As	25%	10 hours studied
8 Bs	40%	8 hours studied
3 Cs	15%	5 hours studied
1 D	5%	1 hour studied
3 Fs	15%	0 hours studied

STUDENTS' GRADES

Grades	Number of Students	Percentage	Avg. Hours Studied
As	5	25	10
Bs	8	40	8
Cs	3	15	5
Ds	1	5	1
Fs	3	15	0

STUDENTS' GRADES

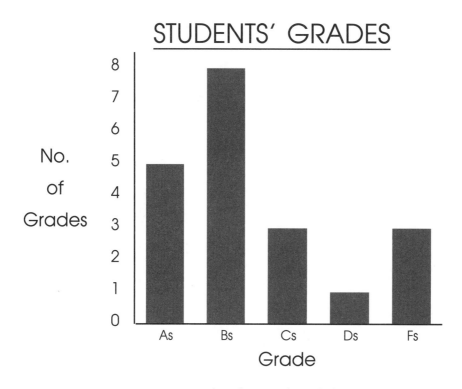

Teaching the Scientific Method

STUDENTS' GRADES — HOURS STUDIED

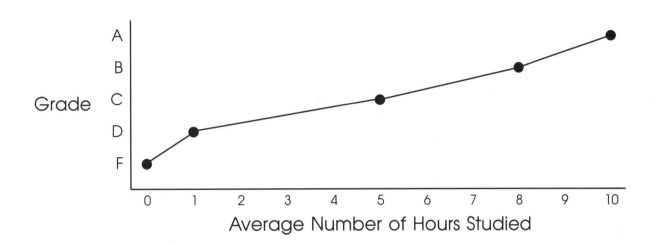

STUDENTS' GRADES — CLASS DISTRIBUTION

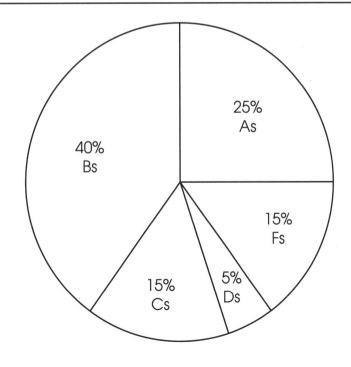

Teaching the Scientific Method

51

Writing the Conclusion

The conclusion is the final step of the scientific method. It must be written in paragraph form and include all of the steps of the scientific method (see page 59). An effective way to teach this step is to have the students perform a guided practice experiment in class. It is good to do one sample experiment with the students, putting every step on the board so they can add this to their notes and refer back to it at any time during the year. Sample experiments that students enjoy are usually those that will allow the class to go outside and enable every student to participate.

IDEAS FOR PRACTICE EXPERIMENTS

1. How many times will the top pop off of a film canister using baking soda & vinegar or water & Alka-Seltzer? (This one definitely must be done outside.)

2. Who in the class can run 30 meters the fastest?

3. Which girl and boy in the class will win the most arm wrestling competitions?

4. Which brand of bubble gum will blow the biggest bubble?

5. Who can stand on their head the longest?

6. Who in the class can shoot the most free throws in 10 tries?

7. What is the order that the liquids will stack from least dense to most dense?

8. Who in the class can hit the softball the farthest?

9. Do daisies grow better with direct or indirect sunlight?

10. Which team will win the most times out of 5 playing tug-of-war?

Sample Experiment Write-Up

POP YOUR TOP OFF

Problem: How many times will the top pop off of a film canister using water and Alka-Seltzer?

Research: When water and Alka-Seltzer come in contact with one another, they undergo a chemical reaction in which CO_2 gas is released. When this gas is contained in a film canister, it will blow the top off.

Hypothesis: If I test to see how many times the top will pop off the film canister, then it will be 6 times.

Materials List:
1. 1 film canister with a tight-fitting top
2. 200 ml of water
3. 3–5 Alka-Seltzer® tablets
4. paper towels
5. tape
6. a partner

Procedure:

1. Tape 1 Alka-Seltzer under the top of the film canister.

2. Fill the canister $\frac{1}{2}$ full of water.

3. Tightly place the top on the film canister.

4. Holding the top and the bottom, shake up and down for about 10 seconds.

5. Release the top.

6. Have your partner retrieve the top and put it back on the film canister.

7. Repeat steps 4–6 until all the Alka-Seltzer and gas is used. (You may refill the film canister with water at any time.)

8. Use the paper towels to dry off the canister before taping another Alka-Seltzer to the lid.

9. Repeat the experiment at least 3 times; record the number of pops for each trial.

Teaching the Scientific Method

Data:

TOP POPS

TESTS CONDUCTED	NUMBER OF POPS
Test one	3 pops
Test two	5 pops
Test three	10 pops

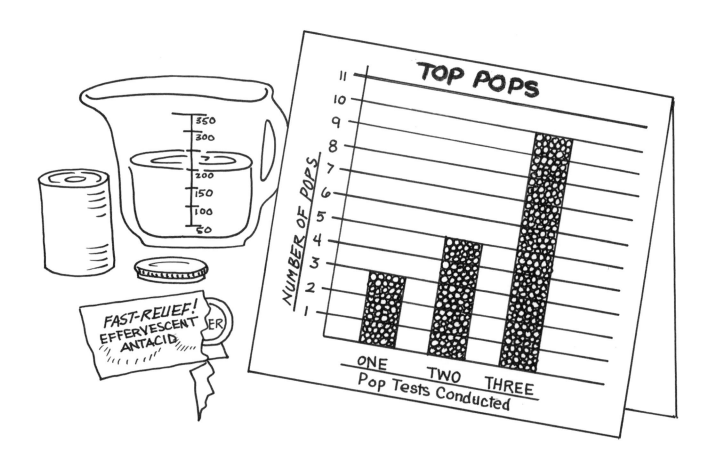

Sample Conclusion:

My hypothesis was not correct because I said the top would pop off 6 times and it did not. It popped off 3 times in the first test, 5 times in the second test, and 10 times in the third test. However, if I calculate the average of the 3 tests, the result is 6 times.

The variable I was testing was the number of times the top would pop off of the canister. Variables I controlled in this experiment were the type of canister used, the amount of water added, the amount of Alka-Seltzer used, and how long I shook the container. Variables I could not control were how high the top flew, how far the top flew, how long it took my partner to retrieve the top, how much water came out with the gas, and if the Alka-Seltzer flew out with the gas. I could not control these variables because they all depended on the amount of gas building up inside the container.

A few extensions of this experiment, or examples of what I could have done differently, are to use baking soda and vinegar instead of water and Alka-Seltzer, or to combine all of these ingredients at once. I also could have tested and recorded how high or how far the top popped off, instead of the number of pops. Lastly, I could have used more Alka-Seltzer and more water with each test.

One concept this experiment taught me was that Alka-Seltzer and water produce a chemical reaction. Another concept I learned was that the production of bubbles indicates a gas is present. I also learned that this chemical reaction can get rather messy if the top is pointed toward you or someone else when it is released. Do not point the top of the canister toward your face.

SCORING GUIDE FOR THE EXPERIMENT WRITE-UP

Title . . . . **2 points**

Labels for each step . . . . . . **14 points** (2 pts. for each step)

Problem . . . . **4 points** (2 pts. if it is written in question form,
and 2 pts. if it is a testable problem and not a
demonstration, model, or research)

Research . . . . **10 points**

Hypothesis . . . . **4 points** (2 pts. for using an "If . . . , then . . ." statement,
and 2 pts. if it relates to and clarifies the problem)

Materials List . . . . **10 points** (5 pts. if it is numbered and written in list form, and
5 pts. if all materials and amounts are included)

Procedure . . . . **10 points** (5 pts. if it is numbered and written in list form, and
5 pts. if the directions are clear, precise, and detailed)

Data . . . . **20 points** (4 pts. each for two different graphics, and 12 pts. if
they are done correctly, complete with title and any
necessary labels)

Conclusion . . . . **26 points**
1st paragraph (7 pts.)—2 pts. for telling if the hypothesis was right or wrong, and
5 pts. if the data is fully explained
(If hypothesis was wrong, tell why.)

2nd paragraph (7 pts.)—1 pt. for identifying the independent variable
3 pts. for listing all controlled variables
3 pts. for listing all variables that could not be controlled

3rd paragraph (6 pts.)—Lists at least two extensions—3 pts. each

4th paragraph (6 pts.)—Explains at least two concepts learned from the
experiment—3 pts. each

This scoring guide may be given to students and parents to inform them of what is expected when conducting and writing up experiments.

REVIEW, TESTS,

and

PROJECTS

Weekly Journal Entries

If your curriculum does not include many tests or homework grades, use weekly journal entries to help students review concepts and collect extra grades. Write the entry on the board before class, and allow students to use their notes to complete the answer in the first five minutes of the session. After everyone has completed the assignment, go over the answer as a class. One journal entry per week, worth 25 points, gives the students an opportunity to make 200 points for the grading period. Require students to write exactly what is written on the board, date it, and answer the question correctly. If they have the wrong answer, they may correct it when the class reviews the answer together.

Some suggestions for journal entries are:

1. List the steps of the scientific method, in the correct order.

2. How should a problem be written?

3. How should a hypothesis be written?

4. How should the materials list and procedure be written?

5. Write a hypothesis for the following problem.

6. Why is it important to write clear, precise, and detailed directions for the procedure?

7. What has been your favorite activity this week and why?

8. List the 5 ways we make observations.

Notes on the Scientific Method

1. **Problem**—written in question form (must be testable); test only one variable at a time

2. **Research**—background information about your experiment from another source; about one to two paragraphs is sufficient; written in paragraph form

3. **Hypothesis**—what you predict will happen; must be written as an "If . . . , then . . ." statement before the experiment is conducted

4. **Materials List**—list and number all materials in list form; include amounts

5. **Procedure**—list and number all steps in list form; must include details

6. **Data**—charts, tables, graphs, pictures; must include at least two different forms

7. **Conclusion**—longest portion of the write-up; must be written in paragraph form

    A. Tell if your hypothesis was correct or incorrect, and explain all of your data/results. If your hypothesis was incorrect, discuss what might have caused it to be so.

    B. Discuss your variables (independent variable—factor that is being tested; dependent variable—changes that result from the independent variable); explain what you were testing for (independent variable); discuss everything you controlled; discuss everything you could not control; discuss dependent variables; use the terms **independent variable** and **dependent variable** in discussions

    C. List at least two extensions. Explain what you could have done differently (possibly a different variable to test)

    D. Explain at least two concepts you learned from conducting your experiment. (Give at least two.)

All experiments should be testable—not research, a survey, demonstration, or model. Use at least three different samples in your test or perform the experiment at least three different times to get more accurate results.

Some experiments allow you to use CONTROLS. Such an experiment uses a separate group to compare with your test group. For example, if you test to see if cigarette smoke affects household plants, then you should have a CONTROL experiment that is not subject to any smoke but is otherwise identical to your experimental group in every way. If you use a CONTROL, be sure to discuss it in paragraph B of your conclusion.

SCIENTIFIC METHOD VOCABULARY & DEFINITIONS

_____ 1. temperature scale used in the metric system

_____ 2. experiment group without a variable

_____ 3. amount of mass per unit of volume

_____ 4. what you think will happen in an experiment

_____ 5. instrument used for measuring mass

_____ 6. basic unit of volume in the metric system

_____ 7. basic unit of mass in the metric system

_____ 8. amount of matter in an object

_____ 9. basic unit of length in the metric system

_____ 10. common system of measurement, especially among scientists

_____ 11. display of a scientific model that simply shows how something works

_____ 12. instrument used to measure volume of liquids and irregularly shaped objects

_____ 13. basic steps used by scientists in solving problems

_____ 14. most logical explanation for events that occur, although unproven

_____ 15. factor being tested in an experiment

_____ 16. measure of the gravitational pull on an object

_____ 17. information gathered during an experiment

_____ 18. scientific information gathered through observations, surveys, etc.

_____ 19. amount of space an object occupies

_____ 20. scientific test in which data is gathered/compared with the use of a variable and often a control

Celsius	experiment	mass	theory
control	graduated cylinder	meter	triple beam balance (TBB)
data	gram	metric system	variable
demonstration	hypothesis	research	volume
density	liter	scientific method	weight

SCIENTIFIC METHOD STUDY GUIDE

1. Differentiate between a demonstration, model, research, and test.

2. Know all the steps of the scientific method and how each should be written.

3. Explain the importance of giving clear, precise, and detailed directions for the procedure.

4. Know the 5 ways to make observations.

5. Know how to pick out key words in a problem to research.

6. Know how to write a hypothesis correctly using an "If . . . , then . . ." statement.

7. Know how to convert units in the metric system.

8. Know the instruments and units that are used when measuring length, mass, and volume (regularly and irregularly shaped objects).

9. Know how to read a triple beam balance, graduated cylinder, and meterstick or metric ruler.

10. Know how to calculate volume for a regularly shaped object and an irregularly shaped object.

11. Know how to calculate density (Density = Mass/Volume) and speed (Speed = Distance/Time).

12. Know how to construct a chart, bar graph, line graph, and pie graph. Know how to calculate percentages for a pie graph.

13. Know how to find and list densities from most dense to least dense and least dense to most dense.

14. Know the difference between mass and weight.

15. Know what an independent variable is and how to identify it.

Name_____ Date_____

SCIENTIFIC METHOD TEST A

1. How is a problem written? _____

_____

_____

2. Determine if each is a demonstration, research, or test.

   A. "How do you make molecule models?" _____

   B. "Which types of foods contain starch?" _____

   C. "How far away is lightning?" _____

   D. "What causes mold to grow on bread?" _____

   E. "How does a volcano work?" _____

3. Given the problem "Which type of fruit tree in Kentucky produces the most fruit?",
   circle the word(s) that you would research before conducting this experiment.

4. Write a hypothesis for the following problem:
   "Which brand of laundry detergent is best for getting rid of stains: Cheer, Tide, or All?"

   _____

   _____

5. List the 5 ways to make observations.

   A. _____

   B. _____

   C. _____

   D. _____

   E. _____

6. How should the materials list be written? What should be included?

_____

Scientific Method Test A, continued

7. Why is it important to give clear, precise, and detailed directions when writing the procedure?

_____

_____

8. When you see bubbles in a reaction, it is an indication that a _____ is present.

9. Convert the following metric units:

   A.   65.78 g = _____ Kg   D. 43.2 cm = _____ dm

   B.   79 Dag = _____ mg   E.   250 m = _____ Hm

   C. 0.4758 Kl = _____ L

10. List which instrument and unit of measurement would be used for the following measurements:

   A. mass of an object   _____   _____

   B. volume of regular shape _____   _____

   C. depth of a barrel   _____   _____

   D. volume of irregular shape_____   _____

11. What would be the volume of an object
    that raised the water level of a graduated
    cylinder from 157 ml to 183 ml?   _____

12. Calculate the volume of a regularly shaped
    object with measurements of 3cm x 2cm x 5cm. _____

13. Draw a pie graph displaying the
    following information (include a title):
    18.5% of the students have brown eyes,
    25% have green eyes,
    32.5% have blue eyes, and
    24% have hazel eyes.

Scientific Method Test A, continued

14. Calculate the speed of climbing a 27-meter hill in 3 seconds.   _____

15. Calculate the density of an object with a volume of 10 ml and mass of 60.5 g.   _____

16. List the following from most dense to least dense: _____
    d = 1g/ml, d = 1.9g/cm³, d = 1.08g/ml, and d = 0.95g/ml.   _____
                                                                _____
                                                                _____

17. For the following, go to the instruments set up on the demonstration tables
    and record the reading in the space provided below:

    A. mass of the apple   _____

    B. length of the pencil   _____

    C. volume of water   _____

18. What is the difference between mass and weight?

    _____

    _____

19. How many paragraphs should be written for the conclusion of an experiment?

    _____

    _____

20. Based on the problem, "Which brand of bubble gum will allow you to blow the biggest
    bubble?", what is the independent variable you are testing?

    _____

Name_____ Date_____

SCIENTIFIC METHOD TEST B

A. Multiple Choice

1. The first step of the scientific method is _____ .
   a. hypothesis
   b. materials list
   c. problem
   d. conclusion

2. Which is a way to make observations _____ ?
   a. smell
   b. taste
   c. sight
   d. all of the above

B. Fill in the blanks with the following words:

triple beam balance (TBB)	graduated cylinder	metric ruler
meters	liters	grams

1. You use a _____ to measure length of an object,

   and the basic units are _____.

2. You use a _____ to measure mass of an object,

   and the basic units are _____.

3. You use a _____ to measure volume of an irregularly-shaped object,

   and the basic units are _____.

Scientific Method Test B, continued

C. Make a bar graph with the following information.
   (Include a title and label each axis.)

When a survey was taken, we found out that several students in our class own dogs.
Sarah has 4 dogs, Tyler has 2 dogs, Kim has 1 dog, and Jacob has 2 dogs.

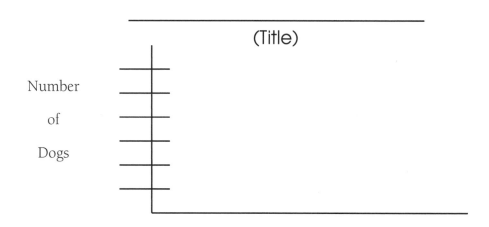

(Title)

Number

of

Dogs

Names of Students

D. Complete the pie graph
   by writing the percentages
   in the correct places.

   50%, 25%, 15%, 10%

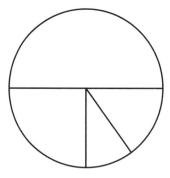

E. Go to the instruments set up in
   the room; read and record the
   measurements for the following:

   A. mass of the apple   _____

   B. length of the pencil   _____

   C. volume of water   _____

Teaching the Scientific Method

©Incentive Publications, Inc., Nashville, TN.

OPEN-RESPONSE QUESTION

Instructions: The following question is about neutralizing an acid. It is designed to test your knowledge of this subject and of experiment designs. Answer all parts of the question completely.

Last week you helped your neighbor clean her basement floor. Since the floor was concrete, you knew that it would take a strong acid such as HCl to remove all the stains from the floor. However, your neighbor's concern was how to get all the acid up once the floor was cleaned. She suggested washing it off with water.

    A. Tell why water would not be the best solution to the problem.

_____

_____

_____

_____

    B. Design a test that will prove to your neighbor that the acid has been neutralized.

_____

_____

_____

_____

    C. Explain how you know the test you designed in part B will work.

_____

_____

_____

_____

RUBRIC for "Neutralization" Open-Response Question

CRITERIA	NOVICE (11.6 pts. each)	APPRENTICE (13.3 pts. each)	PROFICIENT (15 pts. each)	DISTINGUISHED (16.6 pts. each)
Tells why water would not be the best clean up solution	☐ Fails to explain or gives limited or wrong information	☐ Attempts to explain but needs more information	☐ Explains that water would just dilute the acid, not get rid of it	☐ Clearly explains that water would just dilute the acid ☐ May discuss *ppm or give another example
Includes a problem	☐ Problem is not written in question form ☐ Problem is not testable ☐ Problem does not relate to the experiment	☐ Problem is in question form ☐ Problem may not be testable ☐ Problem somewhat relates to the experiment	☐ Problem is in question form ☐ Problem is testable ☐ Problem relates directly to the experiment	☐ Problem is written in question form and includes detail ☐ Problem is clearly a test ☐ Problem clearly relates to the experiment
Includes a hypothesis	☐ Hypothesis is not written as an *If . . . , then . . .* statement ☐ Hypothesis does not relate to the problem ☐ Hypothesis includes words such as *I think, I predict,* etc.	☐ Attempts to write hypothesis as an *If . . . , then . . .* statement ☐ Attempts to relate hypothesis to the problem ☐ Hypothesis does not include words such as "I think"	☐ Hypothesis is written correctly ☐ Hypothesis relates to the problem ☐ Hypothesis does not include words such as "I think"	☐ Hypothesis is written correctly ☐ Hypothesis clearly relates to the problem ☐ Hypothesis does not include phrases such as "I think"
Includes a materials list	☐ Materials list is not written in list form ☐ Materials list is not numbered ☐ 3 or more materials or amounts are excluded	☐ Attempts to write materials list in list form ☐ Materials list is numbered or bulleted ☐ 2 materials/amounts are excluded	☐ Materials list is written in list form ☐ Materials list is numbered correctly ☐ 1 material or amount may be excluded	☐ Materials list is correctly written in list form ☐ Materials list is correctly numbered ☐ No materials or amounts are excluded
Includes the procedure	☐ Procedure is not written in list form ☐ Procedure is not numbered ☐ Procedure is not clear, precise, and detailed	☐ Attempts to put procedure in list form ☐ Procedure is numbered ☐ Procedure lacks some detail	☐ Procedure is written in list form ☐ Procedure is numbered ☐ Procedure is clear, but may lack one or two details	☐ Procedure is correctly written in list form ☐ Procedure is correctly numbered with numbers ☐ Procedure is very clear, precise, and detailed
Explains the test	☐ Explanation has little to do with the experiment	☐ Attempts to explain the test but lacks full knowledge of the concept	☐ Does a good job explaining the test ☐ Demonstrates a good understanding of acids and bases	☐ Clearly and intelligently explains the test ☐ Uses scientific terminology effectively ☐ May give another example of a neutralization test

*ppm-parts per million

Teaching the Scientific Method

OPEN-RESPONSE QUESTION

Instructions: The following question is about determining the controlled variables of an experiment. It is designed to test your knowledge in this area and your knowledge of the best forms of data for particular experiments. Answer all parts of the question completely.

Josh and Sandy are working on an experiment for school to determine if sunlight is a better source of energy than artificial light to make plants grow taller. Josh thinks they will grow better with the artificial light source, and Sandy thinks sunlight is the better energy source.

A. List all the variables that they will need to control for this experiment.

_____

_____

_____

_____

B. Design and/or describe two different forms of data that would work best with this experiment.

_____

_____

_____

_____

C. Explain why the forms of data you used in part B are the best forms for this experiment.

_____

_____

_____

_____

_____

RUBRIC for "Energy Source for Plants" Open-Response Question

CRITERIA	NOVICE (23.2 pts. each)	APPRENTICE (27 pts. each)	PROFICIENT (31 pts. each)	DISTINGUISHED (33.2 pts. each)
Lists Variables	☐ Lists only 1 variable or attempts a few	☐ Lists at least half of the variables	☐ Lists at least 4 of the variables	☐ Lists at least 5 of the variables ☐ Lists only 4 of the variables but gives a brief explanation for each
Includes 2 forms of data	☐ Includes only 1 form of data or 2 of the same form ☐ Graphs or charts are not set up correctly ☐ Data forms are not the best choices for this experiment	☐ Includes 2 different forms of data ☐ At least one of the 2 is set up or described incorrectly ☐ Data forms are O.K. choices	☐ Includes 2 different forms of data ☐ Both are set up correctly ☐ Choices are good	☐ Includes 2 difficult and different forms of data or includes more than 2 ☐ All are set up correctly ☐ Data forms are clearly the best choices for this experiment
Explains why the forms of data chosen are the best for this experiment	☐ Does not clearly explain why the forms used were the best choices	☐ Attempts to explain why they are the best choices	☐ Gives a good explanation as to why both forms are the best choices	☐ Clearly and specifically explains in detail why the data forms are the best choices ☐ May give examples

For Teacher Reference:

Variables to be listed:

Types of plants

Location of plants

Amount of sunlight and artificial light

Amount of water

Beginning size of plants

Type of soil

Possible data forms:

1. Chart to show record of growth or observations

2. Pictures to show growth at different intervals

3. Bar graph to show comparison of growth

4. Line graph to show change in growth over a period of time

5. Pie graph to show percentages of growth of each plant

Teaching the Scientific Method

AN EFFECTIVE SCIENCE FAIR PROJECT

(Include all three items listed below.)

Experiment

- Complexity—Requires a significant amount of time or involves many complex steps

- Creativity—An idea that has not been seen before or one from another source that has been further developed

- Actual Test—The experiment must be an actual test, performed at least three times or with at least three different samples of materials (e.g., three different brands). It is not a model, demonstration, or research.

Display Board

- Presents the scientific method (all seven steps) with the correct information in the correct order.

- Descriptive title with large letters

- Neatly done—shows time and effort

- Correctness—few errors in punctuation, spelling, capitalization, and/or grammar

- Eye Catching—good color coordination and visual appeal

Log Book

- Has a cover page with the title and a picture relating directly to the experiment. (Participant numbers will be given for identification purposes. Do not write names on display board or cover sheet).

- Each step is correctly completed and written on a separate page in book form.

- Appearance—Neatly done. Book is bound together or stapled.

- Correctness—Few to zero errors in punctuation, spelling, capitalization, and/or grammar.

What You Will Be Judged On

- Follows and displays the scientific method correctly and in correct order

- Complexity of the experiment

- Creativity of the experiment

- Neatness of display board and log book

- Correctness in punctuation, spelling, capitalization, and/or grammar on display board and log book

- Appearance of display board and log book—eye catching; appealing

- Inclusion of a display board, a log book, and experiment (or at least materials used in the experiment)

- Actual test is performed at least 3 times or with 3 different samples of materials

Points and Grade

The grade for this project will be based on the following number of points assigned by the judges.

POINTS	GRADE	POINTS	GRADE
28	100	17	88
27	99	16	86
26	98	15	84
25	97	14	82
24	96	13	80
23	95	12	78
22	94	11	76
21	93	10	74
20	92	9	72
19	91	8	71
18	90	7	70

APPENDIX

WEEKLY LESSON PLAN FORM

Name_____ Date _____

Grade _____ Lesson Title _____

Objective: _____

_____

_____

Monday:

_____
Tuesday:

_____
Wednesday:

_____
Thursday:

_____
Friday:

Materials/Resources: _____

_____

Assessment: _____

_____

Revisions/Reflections: _____

_____

DIFFERENTIATION CHECKLIST

(Checklist may be copied on the back of lesson plan sheets.)

Special Education Modifications

_____ Group Work (allows students to work with peers)

_____ Copy Information (allows students to participate with a modified task)

_____ Work with a partner (allows students to receive one-on-one assistance)

_____ Perform different/simpler task with less material, concrete vocabulary words, etc.

_____ Read directions and/or material individually to student

_____ Read directions and/or material to whole class (does not single them out)

_____ Score assignments based on effort rather than completion

_____ Extra Credit

Other_____

_____

_____

Gifted/Talented Modifications

_____ Group Work (allows students to perform leadership roles)

_____ Projects (allow students to display creativity)

_____ Drawings (allow students to demonstrate artistic abilities)

_____ Journals (allow students to express themselves and their knowledge of content through writing)

_____ Challenging assignments such as higher-order thinking questions, creative projects, research, portfolios, technology assignments

_____ Extra Credit (creates a challenge for overachievers)

Other_____

_____

_____

Teaching the Scientific Method

SAMPLE FIRST WEEK LESSON PLAN
(Designed for 50 minute teaching blocks)

The following is a sample of a week's lesson plan, designed to help you use this book in your own classroom. All handouts mentioned are included in the book (along with answer keys where applicable); in addition, all demonstrations mentioned are further explained on pages 10–15.

This is just a sample selection of activities, and can be modified to better fit your students or subject matter.

Day One:
- Go over the Student Notes on the Scientific Method handout (page 59).
- Discuss the importance of following directions. Distribute "Following Directions" (page 17).
- Have students give specific directions for others to follow (page 18).
- Wrap up with a demonstration. Have students write the specific directions of the demonstration (Can Crush or Balloon in Jar, pages 10–11).

Day Two:
- Discuss the differences between a test, research, demonstration, and model (page 20).
- Discuss how to correctly write the problem under investigation (go over examples and practice with activities on page 21).

Day Three:
- Review and then discuss researching information for an experiment.
- Discuss how to write a hypothesis correctly. (Go over examples.)
- Do prediction activities (pages 27–28).
- Wrap up with a demonstration—show materials and have students predict what they think will happen written in the form of a hypothesis.
- Complete "Practice Writing a Hypothesis" (page 26) for homework.

Day Four:
- Review and go over homework.
- Discuss how to write the materials list (page 29).
- Procedure—Have students give you the directions (one at a time) to actually make a peanut butter sandwich (page 31).
- After completing the activity, discuss the importance of giving clear, precise, and detailed instructions in the procedure.
- For homework, have students write directions from school to their home or another destination.

Day Five:
- Continue working on giving clear/precise directions with paper clip designs (page 32).

JUDGES' RUBRIC

Mark the appropriate box, then tally the number of points received in each category.

CRITERIA	Score of 1 for each item below	Score of 2 for each item below	Score of 3 for each item below	Score of 4 for each item below
Displays the scientific method: (1) Problem, (2) Research, (3) Hypothesis, (4) Materials, (5) Procedure, (6) Data (at least 2 forms), (7) Conclusion	☐ Left out more than one step ☐ More than one step is not in correct order in logbook ☐ Not done correctly ☐ Only one form of data shown	☐ Left out one step ☐ One step is not in correct order in logbook ☐ One section is not done correctly	☐ Has all 7 steps of scientific method ☐ One step may not be in correct order on board ☐ 1 or 2 steps lack a bit of information	☐ Has all steps clearly displayed in log book and on board ☐ All steps are in correct order and easy to follow
Complexity	☐ Simple experiment ☐ Took little time to complete ☐ Very few steps were involved	☐ Simple experiment ☐ Took some time to complete ☐ Several steps were involved	☐ Complex experiment ☐ Required quite a bit of time to complete or ☐ Involves many steps	☐ Very complex experiment ☐ Required lots of time to complete or ☐ Involves lots of steps
Creativity	☐ Simple experiment idea ☐ Seen many times before ☐ Not grade level experiment	☐ Simple idea with some creativity added	☐ Idea may have been seen a few times ☐ Idea is further developed/creative	☐ Idea is truly creative ☐ Idea is original
Neatness & Correctness	☐ Not very neatly done ☐ More than 6 errors in punctuation, spelling, capitalization, or grammar	☐ Neatness is O.K. ☐ 2–3 errors in punctuation, spelling, capitalization, or grammar	☐ Neatly done ☐ No more than 2 grammatical errors in log book or display board	☐ Very neatly done ☐ No more than 1 grammatical error in log book or display board
Eye Catching	☐ Not eye-catching or appealing ☐ O.K. color coordination	☐ Plain/ordinary ☐ O.K. color coordination	☐ Quite eye-catching ☐ Good color coordination	☐ Quickly catches your eye ☐ Extremely nice color coordination
Includes Experiment Log Book Display Board	☐ Missing two of the three items ☐ Log book is not very neat ☐ Steps are not all on separate pages	☐ Missing one of the 3 items ☐ Log book is somewhat neat ☐ Log book or display board missing one of the steps	☐ Display board, log book, and experiment are all displayed	☐ All items are neatly displayed and set up for judges to test
Actual test (Not just research, model, or demonstration)	☐ Not a test ☐ It is a survey, research, model, or demonstration	☐ It is a test ☐ Test performed only once or with only one sample	☐ Definite test ☐ Performed only twice or with only 2 samples	☐ Definite test ☐ Performed at least 3 times or with at least 3 different samples

Participant's Grade _____ Participant's Number _____ Participant's Score _____

Teaching the Scientific Method

Answer Key

Page 23

1. model (a demonstration only if it is shown to erupt)
2. research (a survey)
3. test (allows you to experiment with at least 3 different brands of tissue)
4. demonstration
5. demonstration (This might be turned into a test if different cups or liquids were tested.)
6. test
7. test
8. demonstration (It could be turned into a test if the problem was "How many drops of base will it take to neutralize an acid?".)
9. a model and a demonstration
10. demonstration and model
11. research (survey) This could easily be tested with "Which flavor of gum will last the longest?".
12. demonstration
13. test
14. research
15. research
16. test
17. test.
18. model
19. demonstration
20. research

Page 24

1. model
2. test
3. research, demonstration or model
4. research
5. test
6. research
7. test
8. demonstration, or model
9. test
10. test

Page 48

1. 1 liter
2. one thousandth
3. 1000 grams
4. one thousand
5. volume
6. one hundredth
7. one hundred
8. mass
9. 100 meters
10. ten
11. one tenth
12. length, distance, height, depth
13. Celsius
14. the meter
15. ml, liter, cm^3

Page 60

1. celsius
2. control
3. density
4. hypothesis
5. triple beam balance
6. liter
7. gram
8. mass
9. meter
10. metric system
11. demonstration
12. graduated cylinder
13. scientific method
14. theory
15. variable
16. weight
17. data
18. research
19. volume
20. experiment

Answer Key

Scientific Method Test A

1. as a question/with a question mark

2. Determine if each is a demonstration, research, or test.
    - A. Demonstration
    - B. Test
    - C. Research
    - D. Test
    - E. Demonstration

3. Kentucky, fruit, trees, production

4. If I test which brand of detergent among Cheer, All, & Tide would get rid of stains the best, then it will be (any one brand is acceptable).

5. sight, smell, hear, taste, touch

6. numbered and listed, include amounts

7. so others who want to perform your experiment can follow it exactly without questioning the procedure

8. gas

9. A. 65.78 g = 0.06578 Kg
    B. 79 Dag = 790,000 mg
    C. 0.4758 Kl = 475.8 L
    D. 43.2 cm = 4.32 dm
    E. 250 m = 2.50 Hm

10. A. triple beam balance/gram
    B. meterstick or metric ruler/cm^3
    C. meterstick/meter or cm
    D. graduated cylinder/ml or liter

11. 26ml

12. $30cm^3$

13. ―――――

14. 9m/s

15. 6.05g/ml

16. $1.9g/cm^3$
    1.08g/ml
    1g/ml
    0.95g/ml

17. Answers will vary depending on the measurements of the objects chosen.

18. Mass is the amount of matter in an object, and weight is the amount of gravitational pull on an object. Mass does not change; weight can change.

Class Eye Colors

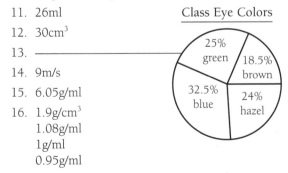

19. The conclusion has 4 paragraphs.

20. The independent variable being tested in the problem is the brand of bubble gum that blows the biggest bubble.

Scientific Method Test B

A. 1. C
   2. D

B. 1. metric ruler/meters
   2. triple beam balance/grams
   3. graduated cylinder/liters

C.

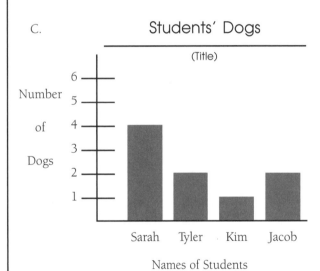

Students' Dogs

D.

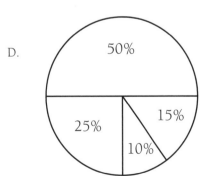

E. Answers will vary according to the measurements of the chosen objects.